To Rekindle Fire

poems by Nigel Wild

for Louise

Earthright Publications

Acknowledgements

Many thanks to all who have encouraged me over the years.
Special thanks to Monica Frisch for all her help and to my
partner Louise Duncan for her support. Also to Tim Jones for
the splendid wood engravings, which he did many years ago,
since when we've completely lost touch. I hope he won't be
too upset that I've used them. If anyone can put me in touch I
would love to make contact again. I think he will be pleased
that they have finally reached the light of day.

Nigel Wild

Front cover: *To Rekindle Fire* linocut by Nigel Wild
Back cover: *Self Portrait (1985)* linocut by Nigel Wild

© Nigel Wild 1999

British Library Cataloguing-in-Publication data
A catalogue record for this book is available from the British Library

Printed on recycled paper by Tyneside Free Press, Newcastle upon Tyne
Published by Earthright Publications
8 Ivy Avenue, Ryton, Tyne & Wear NE40 3PU

ISBN 0 907367 12 7

Contents

Fat Black Slug   5
To Rekindle Fire   6
I Heard We Were At War One Afternoon   10
Night Poacher   12
Will This Year Yet Die And The Next Flare   14
Juggling   16
The Old Green Clock   18
An Ember Amongst Tinder   20
Hill Fort   22
The Many Deaths Of Maria Zuñiga-Figueroa   24
On Each Unpictured Wall   26
Cages   28
Down Brambled Paths   31
In The Wake Of The Train   32
Eyes And Hands For Each Other   34
The Baby Girl   35
Sea Anemones Are Too Beautiful For Bank Accounts   36
Man With A Briefcase   37
Fish Swimming   38
Blakelaw Fusiliers   39
Bees   40
The Bread Oven   42
Walls Of Sinew Bars Of Bone   46
Gaol   48
Jack of Heart?   51
Treasure Trove   52
Low Tide In The Aquarium   53
We Went To Hadamar   54
The Good Cutler   58

Illustrations

To Rekindle Fire linocut by Nigel Wild — front cover

Warplane Overhead wood engraving by Tim Jones — 11

Clown woodcut by Nigel Wild — 17

Tree linocut by Nigel Wild — 23

Moon wood engraving by Tim Jones — 27

Anemone wood engraving by Tim Jones — 36

Tulips in the Bakery linocut by Nigel Wild — 45

Tideline wood engraving by Tim Jones — 53

Cutler linocut by Nigel Wild — 59

Self Portrait (1985) linocut by Nigel Wild — back cover

Fat Black Slug

Have you ever looked at a fat black slug?
That moves slowly across your path
as if it will always be exposed there.

Shiny as pitch
against the dew green carpet
a little yellowed with
the first sprinkling of new sun.

Its four fingered face
distorts and grimaces constantly
as the sense points thrust
tentative spongy feelers
forward to a new world.

The safe extent of which is marked by
the furthest forward feeler
as it holds steady
uninterfered with.

The whole shiny locomotive
imperceptibly pulling forward to that point
with a treacle fluidity beyond grace.

To Rekindle Fire

The warming sun
is reflected by the
the perfect white
cone of the volcano

closing eyes
the hot orange
lava glows behind
the shut lids.

We pass a man
leading a horse
with large hooves
and broad shoulders

to start another
days work. Noble
in spite of a
thousand years

and another
whole life
of subservience
to man with reins.

We pass by
the carabineros
and the huge
hacienda de Rupanco.

We pass campesinos
and are humbled
by their grace and
simplicity of their homes.

It is still early;
workers with toolboxes
and schoolchildren
not long from sleep

share the bus
we rose early for.
Emerging from the
warmth of down

to rekindle fire
from last nights
embers, with a few
sticks of driftwood

lying in great
piles of bleached
remnants at
highwater.

Lips close to ash;
an ancient ritual.
A hurried whispering
confession of sins.

Please catch quickly
and purify us
or at least scorch
stale mouths with coffee.

The orange tongues
flicker an uncertain
light into the
unfolding dawn.

At the waters edge
scooping stars, the pan
eddying mists
on a black suface.

Scattered things gathered
and stuffed in bags
the dust of exploited
workers gathered and scattered

on water suspended
in licking flames.
Stars evaporate with heat
and light of The Big Fire.

Between the tasks
of waking and breaking camp
we take sips and
know we are risen.

I Heard We Were At War One Afternoon

I heard we were at war one afternoon
from Kate who works in the teashop.
I was out in the garden
transplanting strawberry runners.

A few moments before
a war-plane had screeched overhead.
It was an omen.
We are at war.

At first I was amused
and then angry.
I plunged my hands into the soil,
the soil soothes anger.

The soil gives life;
care for it, till it,
things will grow.
There will be enough.

In war we forget about these things.
We forget, and there is war.
In war, soil becomes land.
Land is strategic.

Night Poacher

Sharp wind across the brittle leaf
could betray or mask a cracking twig
could communicate your musk
or bring fragrance on a palm.

Singing sap from log-spires drinks
the moisture in the peat
gives spring to turf
which makes soft determined feet.
Wrapped in burnished leather of their boots.

Drum drum, the dull thuds ripple
to the sentry branch.
Wise eared tawny hoots
a warning to the forest thick- as- thieves.
In dens and alleyways heckles spike
stilettos flash from furry sleeves.

For frozen moments liquid senses flood
rustles read the tarot down a silent horn.
Quick hearts in hiding wait for blood
Unfolding drama in a moon.
Elastic stealth steps: beneath a hood.

Fur and scale, feather, flesh
in their knowing silence wait
refusing to be feast or sacrifice or bait.
Shadows promise secrets; the unknown.

Rush, shriek; the still warm echo.
Deaths dagger grates upon a bone.
Flurry, fluff, blood and flesh torn.
The Night Poacher stalks.
Whose silent corpse shall decorate the dawn?

Will This Year Yet Die And The Next Flare

Will this year yet die
and the next flare
kindling green from the embers
of a forest fire.
Boot licking flames
hot orange and yellows
raging for weeks.

Walk through the inferno
warmed but unburned.
Paths paved with copper and gold
melted from a green ore
by the furnace of summery noons.

Clinker limbs
flame-quenched and gilt-stripped
stand stoic and defiant
of gales and numb frosts
which lay siege the wintry months
uprooting and strangling where they might.

'Til the cavalry sun
to a silent bugle
storms a hill
and the slight warm breath
breathes longer each daily dawn.

Hidden embers feel arson tongues
stir their slumbering mouths
to yawn; farewell!
To hibernating dark.
To suckle the sun and utter
first words of green spark.

Juggling

Juggling with
time and love
and oneself.

Holding for
an instant
letting go.

An economy
of movement
or baubles on a shelf.

17

The Old Green Clock

The sugar-baby dances in the wind
down the back lane
into the yard and out again.
Over the clothes-line
and the telephone wire
in front of the opposite window
reflecting our house and our window.

Above the gutter and the roof slates.
The sugar-baby dances in the wind.
A mile and ten minutes away
from the dandelion clock
all but shed of its time.
A season's long hours
torn away in a moments gust.

Cocked escapement wheels, scattered
to far corners and beds of dust,
to tick a silent cadence through the year
until the bell rings alarm
and slides a movement on its jewels
which springs an arm
and the Big Hand
pulls a helix from its coil.

To strike the hour of rising
out of soil
and into the first hour
of the first day
of the old green clock;
a pendulum swinging
between thistle and thick dock.
Thick dock
thick dock
thick dock.

An Ember Amongst Tinder

Kindling casually collected
from around the hearth ignites
after a slight smoky pause.

Thicker winter windfalls
are dry enough to crack
sharply when broken.

We have smoke and some flame
followed by flame and some smoke.
Flame disappears in sunlight.

The pot is suspended.
Finger thick pieces of ash
are enough to bring it to the boil.

A few sage leaves cast
on the water
impart flavour for a bevy.

Suitable for such an occasion
sat cross-legged
watching the fire, the drifting smoke.

Listening to birdsong, tree rustle
watching the clouds go by:
the shadows lengthen.

Observing Jack's wide-eyed surprise
at the fire lighting ritual
the dancing flame and crackle.

Everything new in the garden
Jack equally miraculous: a bud bursting
an ember amongst tinder.

Hill Fort

A gathering of rocks
in the mist, listening for curlews.
Distantly water tumbles.

Wing flaps emerge and recede.
Bleating; braying, waft
on the edge of a faint breeze.

Maybe the calf's response is an echo
maybe silence lingers amongst rocks
lichens stoic presence softens.

Grasses fruited with
a harvest of water droplets
perfect seed of an identical source.

Shimmering with light
even in the greyness.
A place peopled with previous tongues.

Which never tasted our chocolate
and we never the bitter of their ale
or the grain of their bread.

Our language barren as the hills
all but stripped of the trees
which were their wealth.

The pattern of our syllables
echoes on the granite
their vowels compressed in the peat.

The Many Deaths Of Maria Zuñiga-Figueroa

Hospital des ninos, Roberto de Rio. Santiago
Sin nombres (without name)
in their tiny cots
usually their deaths come soon.
Abandoned from the Barrios.
Too thin to survive.

Too little trickles down to them.
Maria Zuñiga-Figueroa
sees them through glass
from where she works in the Lab.
She fills in their forms
arriving and leaving.

Sin nombres leave stiff
thrown in mass graves.
She sees them coming and going
each week.
After a while she can bear it no more.
Fabricating a family
filling in the forms with their details.

Passes round a hat
and with the few pesos
buys a small grave
some flowers
a wooden cross.
She walks to the cemeterio
with a small box.

Each weeks tragic ritual
a sadness growing
with the line of small graves.
Grief in inverse proportion to their size.

Sometimes she is their mother
sometimes they have her name.
How gracious and frequent
the many deaths
of Maria Zuñiga-Figueroa.

On Each Unpictured Wall

On each unpictured wall
you're subtly impregnated.
Residual narcotic
alters perceptions
from all angles
and soft pillows.

Introspective cups
in sympathetic cafés
allow thought to hang
like cigarette smoke
before it dissipates,
seeping into the surroundings
and the fabric.

The black notebook
blankly pleading decoration
is a discordant diary.
Never as beautiful as I could wish.
Oh! but the beauty I have seen
and not regretted
the passing of it: unrecorded.

Cages

The sad pigeons outside
eating off our crusts
their wing flaps beyond bars
tantalise; and stare

into our cages
at these tragic creatures
slothful in inappropriate
surroundings: disengaged.

At various times
a small flurry of activity
they are let out
for the rituals of emptying

and filling buckets and bowls
then slam again
the arid cell without
a scrap of grass!

At feeding times
they are trained to
follow in line, take a
tray and have it filled

then back again to
the cage. A flicker of
interest; cut with
disgust and despair.

Food forced with greed
and cast aside with
contempt. This chimps
tea party a pathetic

highlight to another
slow day passing
from one routine
opening of the cage

to another closing
of the impenetrable door.
Sometimes at night
two large males

scream at each other
from cage to cage
a bitter litany of
provocation to satisfy

some unknown need
for domination.
Daytime brings
glances and asides

during the ritual
feedings and slop outs.
Subdued threats of
imminent pain and awful death.

The others passive in
their observation of this
contest, indifferent but
satisfied, their frustrations

are acted out vicariously
by these swollen gladiators
held in their many
cages of imprisonment.

Down Brambled Paths

Dusty with feet of mothers, siblings,
wheels of old perambulators, slung regal.
Rich as clusters of fruit down brambled paths.

Austerity was another childhood: berries glimmering memories.
Red stained, sticky as children; carefree, cared for.
Round and bright as quartz in dry-stone walls.

Gritstone: rough on hands. Hedges; thorned lessons, tinged.
A hum of bees and winged beasties.
Mesmeric: a dragonfly stops the world.

Rustled leaves are psalms celebrating harvests.
The green year ends; pram wheels turn,
siblings grow out of each others shoes.

The brambled path; become a bus route.
A wide road, proud with large semis
and new cars. Austerity is another childhood.

Children growing up without brambled paths
careless, uncared for. Round and bright as quartz
in dry-stone walls, bulldozed, for hard-core.

InThe Wake Of The Train

Electric
cold steel flight
through wet field
and misted shire
a touch on the brakes
centrifuged on a steep bend.

Passing through small towns
you're never quite sure
the sequence of.
From the height of the
embankment
you look down into
acres of tarmac.

With clusters of flat rooved
buildings; shabby now,
never been anything but.
Unremarkable men walk
to their second hand cars
carrying cheap briefcases.

They have forgotten their
bold ambitions;
are now thankful
for the opportunity
to drive throughout the county
and sincerely imitate
meaningful discussions.

I am one of those men.
Glancing up at the train
I see myself through your eyes
fleetingly:
believe me
my bold ambitions are still intact
crumpled between
reports and spreadsheets.

From the height of the
embankment
you look down
I am one of those men.
Glancing up at the train
I see myself
through your eyes.
In the wake of the train
a vacuum.

Eyes And Hands For Each Other

Eyes and hands for each other
a full complement of each
blown to bits one afternoon
whilst the sun shone the battle raged.

In a confused half-hearted way
whilst flowers blossomed and leaves trembled
whilst stones lay implacably
and the earth shuddered.

Fields away cotton ripened
in fluffy bolls, already contracted
by local gins. Then by train
to the smoky port and Liverpool.

To t' mill to spin yarn to weave bandage
in vast loose acres and supply
the unending demands of flesh.
Packed and bound for the same torn fields.

Other hands; deft of sordid practice,
neatly bandage ragged stumps
and hold the remains of punctured eyes
which cry darkness into the absorbent fibre.

The Baby Girl

Thankyou for the Woman
and the baby girl.
Following the boy
will be a hard life
and; equally
no contest.

Your unfolding limbs
apparent fragility
will be sinewy
like your mothers.
You will need
to be resilient
and determined
to keep up with
the brother when
he tries to lose you!

We spent the nine months
you spent inside
not wanting to
want a girl.
We will, no doubt,
spend the next years
trying not to
expect too much.
In the meantime
we're just glad
you're little Elsie.

Sea Anemones Are Too Beautiful For Bank Accounts

Inarticulate machine,
inadequate computer.
Express your wave functions
in terms of sand.
Eroded headlands
are flatfish on Dogger.

Sea Anemones are too beautiful
for bank accounts.
Their tentacles
grip fingers
as if terribly insecure
and, of course, I retreat
refusing to be food or wisdom.

Man With A Briefcase

The man with a briefcase
free-falls from a B-52.
His black umbrella thoughts cast shadows
where rain cannot soak the good earth.
Where sun cannot warm the young seedlings.

The backs of naked children
are pelted with the hard rain
of investment bombs.
Which leech all goodness
into underground vaults
awash with blood and broken bodies
on which the monster feeds.

Transforming everything into plastic effigies
poured into the bowls of golden sun
which the man with a briefcase
steals from hungry children
for his breakfast
before going out into the world once more
with his black umbrella.

To cast further shadows on the children
whose bellies are now swollen.
His feet are in the underground vaults
awash with blood and broken bodies.
He cannot see them for his own belly
bulging under his pin-striped waistcoat.

Fish Swimming

Surprising as a leapt salmon
impossible as a run of falls
but here in this gentle eddy
hopeless for your hungry belly,
aching for your strong curved back.
A mere, parochial, pool fish.
Shadow to a rocky basin.

Fascinated by that which swims,
flattered to be of interest.
Familiar with the passers-by
on their travels and migrations,
wise to their needs, and obliging.
Careful not to be devoured;
we may linger a while; and dance.

Quaff skinsful of Adam's own ale.
Swim idle distance together.
Sad the inevitable parting,
aware of just inconsequence
beyond the pool and the leapt fall,
where lovers rendezvous for sex
and unrestricted ecstasy.

Blakelaw Fusiliers

Their names and character
degree of literacy and disaffection
adorn the bus shelters.
Tradition and veteran refugees
agree on the number of repairs
in the decade.

Only since "The Recruitment"
have work experience boys
lavished austere paint upon them.
To remind bus-queue Mums
their pride is now justified
as borstal boy graduates
repeat the time honoured acquiescence
to the old school tie
around their necks.

They learn a trade
from decorated exponents.
How, with Her Majesty's blessing
to leave an imprint
on the shelters
of colonial estates.

Bees

Bees
wax lyrical
to sepal and stamen
pollen-chat the stalk-head
nods encouragement.
The forage flight
traced steps
morse tap
the drone flock.
Obedient and without sex:
for the queen,
the hive,
the comb,
the very hex.

A magic
beyond the aerodynamic.
Blossom beckons
scented and delicate
glowing aromatic
to the hungry sense.
Sweet nectar
of the lush parts,
cupped sweetly
in fleshy urns.
Drawn discreetly
along the hives capillary
emptied with mechanical satisfaction.
Turned from; casually,
brushing sticky stamens
and dusty anthers.

Launched from a velvet lip
into blue faith.
Drawn to the seething magnet
on a dizzy flight
heavy with juice.
Absorbed easily
into the toiling mass
of worker-artists
producing grubs and honey.
A whole economy
of jelly; and wax
culled by apiarists
for candle makers
and connoisseurs of scented light.

The Bread Oven

This oven is an idea sown
a grain chosen
set for germination
deep in the head-mulch
the rotting vegetation
of half-grown ideas
mown and dug in
for green manure.

Left for the silent, unseen magic
to do its stuff.
With enough moisture
heat and light
gleaned from the piss of cynics
the hands of builders
the eyes of enthusiasts.

Left long enough
for as long as the season is
'til roots emerge
and the growing tip
breaks the earth's crust
and instant recognition
of the light

which fires the engine
which drives the sap
which sucks life
from dark minerals.
Lying still, inert
apparently dead
awaiting the parasite
with indifference

as to whether 'tis greed
or hunger that is fed.
This fired engine
will draw life to give life.
This seed is grown
to flourish to seed
to sow to reap
to mill to flour

to warm leaven
to raise dough
to bake bread
to feed mouths
to speak truth
to eat truth.
Which gives strength
to sowing limbs
to reaping limbs
to threshing limbs.

Which choose grain
to set for germination
deep in the head-mulch
of contradictions
and temptation.
Which might beg
which might plead
to burn the grain
to blacken the seed
and switch out the light
which fires the engine
which drives the sap
which sucks life
from dark minerals.

Walls Of Sinew Bars Of Bone

Town Moor night grass drizzled wet.
Night pilgrim to a morning ocean strides
beneath a moon under a cloud
to twist within the turning tides.

Through pools of light, caves of shadow
past railings, posts and telegraph.
Rainfall hardens; deepens on the month.
Past gardens bricks and sleeping lives
husbands close and distant wives.

Children, warm in simple hopes.
Stir with slightly tortured dreams.
Through curtain chink
a worldly light, thinly, sharply gleams.

Through pools and unimprinted mud
past the pickets' braziers beacon
hail "good luck"(and don't you weaken).
Laden lorries roar and rumble
shanks pony spooks. From silence curses mumble.

Past the depots' lorries, pallets, cases.
Square, corrugated, blank and ugly places.
Taste the moist air and smell the muck-spread field
touch the woven green, sodden black, weather shield.

Beneath this trusty coat a feathered thing
rib to feathered rib and touch the perfect wing.
The beauty of the comfort of a warm breast
against a hard and hungry chest.

Which loves the soaring bird; yet unrisen
tethered, well fed, starved within the man prison.
Walls of sinew bars of bone
forced solitary, forced company; unfree and unalone.

Through the still Bay streets and milk float hum
to the gull-squat fields without a crumb.
Scramble, lift ,flap and angry squawk
to the clumsy plunder of the man-hawk.

Into the blue light and breathe the dawn mist
one last caress and final thoughts are kissed.
Along the prom' to the ancient beach
I tear you from a thick heart, gently reach

high as I can hold, perch upon these broken hands
up and away over the wide sea to New Lands.
Stand for a moment, for the wing flaps to linger
shed the old clothes ; with the unbuttoning finger.

Gaol

I was brought here. It was so civilised
if you resisted they would break your arms.
They lock you up quite pleasantly.
I like the colour of our cells.

We were handcuffed together for the journey
right hand to right hand.
We had difficulty co-ordinating
the metal on our wrists
and breaking the screws head
or garrotting him: I guess.

There are many processes in being processed.
Numbers and lists and statements.
I have a new identity. My old one
renewed with my clothes.

I am allowed a small selection of belongings.
A toothbrush but no toothpaste.
A radio but no battery
you could put it in a sock
(and cause assault and battery!)

Worse it could be used as currency
or contain drugs. Baccy is a problem.
Too much time too little baccy.
Everyone has tattoos
they remind you of yourself
and can't be taken away.

My new clothes more or less fit
although I can't see myself in them.
I slop out when they say "Slop Out"
I go to my cell when they say "Get In".

They wander the landings
with their keys, looking bored.
Some have a sense of humour
some think they're funny.

A piss in the bucket
creates an ammoniacal stench
from years of stale piss; ingrained.
I have a lovely rug on my bed
beautifully woven, green and maroon.

I walk the exercise yard in the wind
and rain and sleet. It is bleak
in shirt sleeves in November.
Talk is of time done, of years to do.

"Do It Tony". They "Do It".
The hard men, the sad, the bitter, the lonely.
Some "Do It" laughing; stoic.
"Do It" day in, day out, year after
fucking bastard fucking year.

At first it is depressing.
Some are lucky, they have something
indomitable, which is infectious.
Life goes on until that far-away day.
Until then all promises are quite convincing.

Jack Of Heart?

Head first into the world
in which
you'll have to stand on your own two feet
We'll help you all we can; but,
these days,
there's no depending on the old trades.
You'd have thought knives and bread
sure fire
certainties for all time,
but no!
The markets are fickle
or worse.
Jack we'll teach you how to
care for
yourself, others, the environment. A
good heart
is all we ask of you.

Treasure Trove

The old man with a stick
and a bag and a rope
combs the tideline

for its treasure.
Picking over the shells
pieces of undone work.

Still beautiful fragments.
The debris of broken creatures
which once; and forever,

combed the tideline
for its treasure.
Picking over the shells

pieces of undone work
the debris of creatures.
Still; beautiful fragments.

Low Tide In The Aquarium

Fish from the dead man's tank.
How strangely tenuous chains entwine;
bubbles aerate gills from pinned sockets.

A green film blurs
images swim through moist eyes:
unblinking a spring wells; gushes silently.

A siphon tube empties the stagnant house
the cycle turns; ebbs
low tide in the aquarium.

We Went To Hadamar

We went to Hadamar today;
we can't go there again.

We followed step by step;
the short walk of those
who came this way before.
From the grey bus
to the shed
and down the wooden corridor.

Imagining their responses
sobs, whispered questions,
uncertainties, stumbling; fear.
As they came very, very near.
From inglorious herding
at clinics, hospitals, kind-of-homes.
To this! Arrival, Asylum? Danger?

The beds promised sleep
a continuation
of the dullest of routines.
From meal to meal and bed to bed.

We followed step by step;
the short walk of those
who came this way before.
From the grey bus
to the shed
and down the wooden corridor.

To the Herr Doktor
and his chilling diagnosis.
One of seventy on a list
to justify the treatment
down the stairs.
One by one they followed;
instructions too they must abide.
Into the cellar
nowhere else to go
and no earthly place to hide.

Invited to a room
discard everything to shower.
Packed tightly in the
cream-tiled chamber
to be dead within the hour.

From the Chamber
from the Gas
from the Extermination.
To a dissecting table
for gold fillings
and removal of body parts.

Wheeled and carried
from one heap to another
to await incineration.
Stuff three corpses in at once
with valuable wood and coal.
Fire baulked at the quantity of flesh
was dampened by flesh
flavoured by flesh:
and slowly burned.
Filled the sky with blackest smoke
which hung over Hadamar
which still clings to Hadamar.
Where people knew
but didn't want to know.

Day after day
month after month
the sky darkened over Hadamar.
Shifts of workers took their turn
piling corpses, burning corpses.
Going to their accommodation,
playing cards, going to the bar,
playing football.Not talking
of the task that demeaned them;
that kept them alive.
Long enough to have a break
in a hotel on Bodensee.

Long enough to complete
the ordered task.
Long enough to celebrate
the ten thousandth corpse
with flowers and songs
and free jugs of beer.

We stood in the extermination chamber.
Imagined a death; and another.
Imagined a room-full of deaths; and another,
but ten thousand deaths
are impossible to grasp.
We wandered 'round the cellar
slowly and in silence,
numbed, appalled.
This is still a hospital,
still a Psychiatric Hospital.
Things could be worse!

We could follow step by step
the short walk of those
who came this way before
from the grey bus
to the shed
and down the wooden corridor.

We went to Hadamar today;
we can't go there again.

The Good Cutler

Four score years ago; into this world
a wit and whetstone came.
And this night of extinguished light
bread and meat are still cleaved
with your good cutlers name.

 On the table of their feast
you are an unknown guest
the "iron", purposeful, in right hand held
you also have caressed.

Eighteen times or more;
generations wisdom to impart.
With keenness of eye and firmness of hand
and trueness of now burst heart.

To fix a confident handle
and hone an edge that's keen
to brightly polish straight flat sides
and control the crude machine.

You had your sparkling times
I have no shadowed doubt.
In the glinting shires sun
with golden bream and rainbow trout.

To base metal you are returned
before the knives you ground are thin
to melt with all the universe
and be re-cast with more purity than sin.

May I remember you
each time I hold a blade
may the cut I make be good
know from you that I am made.